Maquette : David Alazraki

18 rue Barbès, 92120 Montrouge
ISBN : 978-2-7470-8839-8
Dépôt légal : octobre 2017
Loi 49-956 du 16 juillet 1949 sur les publications
destinées à la jeunesse

Imprimé France chez Pollina en septembre 2017 - 82201

www.bd-kids.com

A. Didier et O. Muller

Clément Devaux

Anatole Latuile

Bravo Anatole !

BD KIDS

Tu te dépêches, Anatole? Ça fait cinq minutes que je t'attends! Il est déjà 10h20 et la récré va être finie.

1
Gare à la casse

Anatole lève la tête de son cartable :

– Je ne comprends pas, dit-il à sa copine Henriette. Je suis sûr d'avoir mis ma balle rebondissante au fond de mon sac, hier soir, et elle n'y est plus !

Soudain, il se frappe le front.

– Je me souviens ! Jason me l'a empruntée, ce matin, en venant à l'école. Ma balle doit être dans ses affaires.

Anatole se jette sur la trousse de Jason.

– Elle est là ! s'exclame-t-il, tout content.

Et il lance la balle dans la direction d'Henriette. La balle rebondit contre le tableau, renverse au passage une boîte de craies puis atterrit sur le bureau en faisant tomber les lunettes de la maîtresse.

Henriette se précipite pour les ramasser.

– Tu as de la chance, elles ne sont pas cassées, soupire-t-elle. Je crois qu'on ferait mieux d'aller jouer dans la cour.

– D'accord ! répond Anatole en récupérant sa balle.

Il ferme alors un œil, replie son bras comme un lanceur de base-ball et l'envoie dans le couloir…

Henriette gémit :

– Oh non ! Cette fois, j'ai l'impression que tu as vraiment cassé quelque chose.

Les enfants s'élancent vers la sortie. Le buste de Jules Ferry, qui trônait dans l'entrée de l'école, gît sur le carrelage.

Anatole remet rapidement le buste en place.

– Ouf, il n'a rien de cassé, sauf le nez !

– Mais ça se remarque énormément ! s'écrie Henriette. Surtout qu'il avait le nez long !

Anatole pivote sur lui-même.

– Je vais chercher un tube de colle !

Quelques instants plus tard, Anatole applique le nez dégoulinant de colle au milieu de la figure de plâtre. Satisfait, il recule d'un pas :

– Et voilà !

– Et voilà quoi ? demande Henriette.

Anatole ramasse le nez qui est tombé et le fourre dans sa poche. Il glisse à Henriette :

– Tant pis ! De toute façon, il vaut mieux ne pas le laisser traîner.

– Tu n’as plus qu’à espérer que ça passe inaperçu ! lui chuchote Henriette. En tout cas, tu peux compter sur moi pour rester discrète.

2
Drôle de coïncidence

Après la récréation, les élèves de CM1 retournent en classe. Olympe Fayoli s'arrête devant le buste de Jules Ferry.

– Maîtresse, regardez ! s'écrie-t-elle. Il a perdu son nez. On dirait le sphinx !

Madame Gouloминoff tourne la tête et sursaute :

– Mais il était encore entier, ce matin ! Qui a endommagé ce buste ?

Les élèves se regardent, intrigués, mais personne ne répond. Madame Goulominoff les fait entrer dans la classe.

Elle pose ses poings sur son bureau et balaye du regard les têtes de ses vingt-huit élèves.

– Alors ? reprend-elle, j'attends un aveu.

Anatole porte la main à sa poche. Le nez de plâtre est toujours là. Quelle idée il a eue de le garder… Il aurait mieux fait de le jeter par la fenêtre ! « Pourvu que la maîtresse n'organise pas une fouille », se dit-il.

Justement, madame Goulominoff s'approche de lui d'un air soupçonneux. Anatole sent son cœur accélérer et souhaite de toutes ses forces que quelque chose se produise pour faire diversion.

Au même instant, Naomie Crumble se met à crier.

Anatole se retourne et voit Françoise, la gerboise de la classe, qui bondit dans l'allée en zigzaguant entre les sacs d'école.

– Aidez-moi à l'attraper ! lance la maîtresse d'une voix suraiguë.

Tous les élèves se lèvent. La gerboise, apeurée, fait demi-tour et parvient à se faufiler dans l'armoire de madame Goulominoff.

– Elle va grignoter mes fiches pédagogiques ! s'écrie la maîtresse.

Tandis qu'elle essaie de retrouver les clefs de son armoire, les enfants tentent de forcer la porte. Il faut faire vite : à l'intérieur, on entend des grignotements inquiétants.

Enfin, Jason réussit à faire sauter la serrure à l'aide de son compas et Françoise apparaît dans une dentelle de papier crépon.

Une fois la gerboise dans sa cage, la maîtresse s'affale sur la chaise de son bureau.

– Où en étions-nous ? demande-t-elle, l'air un peu égaré.

La fin de la matinée se déroule sans autre incident. À la cantine, tous les élèves parlent de l'évasion de Françoise.

– Je peux vous dire que ça m'a bien arrangé ! lance Anatole en sortant de sa poche le nez en plâtre et en l'appliquant au milieu de sa figure.

Anatole poursuit :

– Mais le plus étonnant, c'est ce qui m'est arrivé juste après la récréation... Écoutez ça : quand la maîtresse s'est approchée de moi, j'ai souhaité très fort que quelque chose se produise pour me sauver.

– Et c'est là que Françoise s'est évadée ! remarque Jason, intéressé.

Les camarades d'Anatole le regardent, impressionnés.

– Pour être sûr qu'il s'agit d'un superpouvoir, il faudrait vérifier que ça fonctionne à chaque fois…, suggère Achille. Tiens, par exemple, tu pourrais souhaiter échapper au contrôle d'histoire de cet après-midi. Si ça marche, ce sera une preuve !

Henriette intervient :
– Attention, voilà la dame de service !
Anatole ramasse le nez et le fait disparaître d'un geste.

3
Des superpouvoirs ?

Madame Goulominoff ouvre son cartable. Elle fouille dans son sac pendant un moment et fronce les sourcils :

– Mais où sont passées les questions du contrôle d'histoire ?

Anatole regarde Jason d'un air victorieux :

– Elle peut les chercher longtemps ! À mon avis, elles se sont désintégrées !

– Ah ! les voilà ! dit la maîtresse soulagée, en brandissant une liasse de papiers. Elles avaient glissé au fond de mon sac.

– Qu'est-ce que tu disais ? demande Jason à Anatole.

– Rien, rien…

Anatole saisit son stylo d'un air résigné quand la porte de la classe s'ouvre en grand.

La directrice fait irruption dans la pièce. Elle est accompagnée par madame Migeot, la dame de service.

Madame Goulominoff tousse un peu.

– J'avais commencé à mener mon enquête ce matin sur cette histoire de statue et…

– De toute façon, nous tenons le coupable ! coupe la directrice. Madame Migeot l'a vu jouer avec le nez de Jules Ferry à la cantine. Il s'agit d'Anatole Latuile.

La directrice ordonne :

– Prends tes affaires et suis-moi.

Anatole plie bagages et lui emboîte le pas. Dans son bureau, la directrice lui fait la morale…

La directrice se lance dans des explications compliquées sur les actions de Jules Ferry.

Anatole écoute d'une oreille distraite et sursaute soudain quand la directrice tape sur son bureau.

– Pour la peine, ordonne-t-elle, tu copieras cinquante fois sa biographie* dans le dictionnaire.

* C'est l'histoire de sa vie.

À la sortie de l'école, tout le monde se rassemble autour d'Anatole.

– Elle ne m'a pas loupé, soupire-t-il. J'ai eu une punition énorme ! Copier cinquante fois la biographie de Ferry. Ça va me prendre au moins six heures !

– Oui, mais tu as évité l'interro d'histoire, dit Jason, et elle était terrible !

– C'est vrai ça, reprend Achille. Ton superpouvoir a fonctionné !

Anatole a soudain les yeux qui brillent.

Henriette regarde Anatole et fait une petite moue :

– Moi, à ta place, je ferais quand même la punition, par précaution.

Anatole lance son sac sur son épaule.

– Tu n'es pas encore habituée à mon super-pouvoir, Henriette, mais tu vas finir par t'y faire.

4

Ça se confirme

Après avoir dit au revoir à sa bande de copains, Anatole rentre chez lui. Il caracole sur le chemin en faisant tourner son sac dans les airs.

Il réfléchit à plusieurs choses agréables qui pourraient l'attendre chez lui.

– Voyons voir, dit-il à mi-voix. Je pourrais souhaiter un supergoûter ? Échapper à la douche ? Ou alors que ma chienne me fasse la fête quand je rentre ?

Il claque soudain dans ses doigts.

– Non, j'ai une meilleure idée ! Ce que j'aimerais avoir, c'est un tas de nouvelles cartes Cap'tain Startruc !

À peine a-t-il passé la grille du jardin que des aboiements retentissent. Sa chienne déboule en trombe et manque de le renverser. Elle le regarde, la langue pendante.

– Tu sais quoi ? lui susurre Anatole à l'oreille, j'ai un don extraordinaire ! Si un jour tu ne veux pas faire un vaccin chez le vétérinaire, tu n'as qu'à me le demander. Je te résous le problème en quelques secondes.

Princesse envoie une grande léchouille sur la main d'Anatole alors qu'il entre dans la maison.

Madame Latuile apparaît dans les escaliers de la cave.

– Je fais le grand ménage de la rentrée, lui lance-t-elle, et j'ai retrouvé plein de choses qui t'appartiennent derrière la baignoire. Je les ai mises sur la table de la cuisine.

Dans la cuisine, Anatole découvre trois vieilles BD jaunies et tachées, une roulette de roller et… un paquet de cartes de Startruc qui sentent le moisi.

Anatole monte dans sa chambre :

– Pour moi, c'est comme si ces cartes étaient neuves… Même quand on sait qu'on va recevoir ce que l'on a souhaité, on est surpris !

À l'école, le lendemain matin, Anatole avance crânement dans le couloir, sûr de l'efficacité de ses pouvoirs.

Anatole s'installe à sa place.

– Où sont les lignes que j'ai commandées ? se demande-t-il.

Il tâtonne dans son casier et en ressort bientôt une liasse de feuilles recouvertes d'une écriture soignée :

Après avoir demandé la permission, Anatole sort de la classe pour aller remettre sa punition. Il fait un V de victoire à Jason, juste avant de refermer la porte.

Bientôt la nouvelle fait le tour de la classe : ça ne fait plus de doute, Anatole a un don extraordinaire. À la récréation, les élèves s'agglutinent autour de lui.

Anatole recule pour échapper à ses camarades qui le pressent. Mais Naomie le rattrape :

– Ma mère ne veut pas que j'aille à une boum. Tu pourrais souhaiter qu'elle change d'avis ?

Un autre élève bouscule Naomie pour s'approcher d'Anatole.

Jason fait le service d'ordre.

Naomie prend soudain un air rêveur :

– À ta place, je demanderais de vivre une grande histoire d'amour passionné.

– Bonne idée ! répond Anatole en lui faisant un clin d'œil.

5
Ah, l'amour !...

De retour en classe, les enfants découvrent leur maîtresse qui discute avec la directrice. Elle agite furieusement devant elle la punition que lui a rendue Anatole.

– Un élève qui ne fait pas sa punition lui-même ! fulmine-t-elle.

La maîtresse hoche la tête.

– Pour moi, c'est une écriture de fille ! reprend la directrice. Qu'en pensez-vous ?

Madame Goulominoff examine la feuille couverte de lignes et donne son verdict.

– En tout cas, ce n'est pas l'écriture d'Anatole Latuile.

– Qui a fait cette punition à ta place ? demande la directrice en foudroyant le garçon du regard.

Anatole baisse les yeux, gêné.

La directrice et la maîtresse se consultent rapidement. Il n'y a vraiment rien à tirer de ce garçon !

– Qui a fait la punition ? demande madame Goulominoff à l'ensemble de la classe.

Les élèves baissent la tête. Mais, soudain, à la surprise générale, une petite voix se fait entendre.

Anatole écarquille les yeux. Incroyable ! Henriette vient de lever la main… et elle est blanche comme un linge.

– J'ai fait la punition à la place d'Anatole, avoue-t-elle. Mais il n'était pas au courant…

La directrice fronce les sourcils.

À midi, Anatole et Henriette ne sont pas à la cantine. Entre les élèves de la classe, les discussions vont bon train.

À cet instant, Anatole apparaît.

– Ne me parlez plus jamais de superpouvoirs, dit-il sombrement en s'asseyant à la table de ses copains. Ma punition a doublé, je vais y passer mon week-end.

– C'est quand même dommage, soupire Ulysse. On commençait vraiment à croire à ton don. Mon grand frère, qui est en cinquième, voulait te rencontrer…

Henriette, les joues roses, arrive à son tour dans le réfectoire.

Naomie soupire :

– Aaah ! l'amour… Des fois, ça vous fait faire n'importe quoi !

Le visage de Jason s'éclaire.

– Mais tiens ! dit-il à Anatole. Si Henriette a fait tout ça par amour pour toi, ça confirme que tu as vraiment un don exceptionnel ! Tu te souviens de ce que tu as souhaité, ce matin, à la fin de la récréation ?

Achille se met à pouffer de rire.

Anatole manque de s'étrangler.

– Mais je ne pensais pas à Henriette… je la connais depuis le CP !

Jason regarde Anatole avec un air d'évidence :

– Tu te rends compte de tous les risques qu'elle a pris pour toi ?

– Tu as raison, Jason ! s'exclame Ulysse.

Ulysse se tourne vers Anatole :

– D'ailleurs, ça me fait penser que j'ai perdu mon cahier de contrôle, il y a deux jours. Tu pourrais peut-être le retrouver ?

– Et moi, j'ai un problème avec ma grand-mère, ajoute Olympe. Tu peux sûrement m'aider.

– À ce propos, tu pourrais aussi demander des cartes de Startruc pour moi ? demande Jason.

Anatole se passe une main sur le front.

FIN

THE BROC Y

b
Thoughts and Prayers

BROCKHAMPTON PRESS
LONDON

This edition published 1996 by Brockhampton Press, a member of Hodder Headline PLC Group

ISBN 0 86019 238 6

Printed in the UK

Contents

Book of Thoughts and Prayers

Sarah Flower Adams 1805–48

From *Nearer, My God, to Thee*

Yet in my dreams I'd be
Nearer, my God, to Thee,
Nearer to Thee.

Aeschylus 525–456 BC

Bestow, O God, this grace on us, that in the school of suffering we should learn self-conquest, and through sorrow, even if it be against our will, learn self-control.

Alcuin 735–804

Eternal Light, shine into our hearts,
Eternal Goodness, deliver our thoughts from evil,
Eternal Power, support our prayer,
Eternal Wisdom, enlighten the darkness of our ignorance,
Eternal Pity, haver mercy upon us;
that with all our heart and mind and soul and strength we may seek thy face, and be brought by thine infinite mercy to thy holy presence; through Jesus Christ our Lord.

St Anselm 1033–1109

O Lord our God, grant us grace to desire thee with a whole heart, that so desiring thee we may seek and find thee, and so finding thee may love thee, and loving thee, may hate those sins which separate us from thee, for the sake of Jesus Christ.

We bring before you, O Lord, the griefs and perils of peoples and nations; the necessities of the homeless; the helplessness of the aged and weak; the sighings of prisoners; the pains of the sick and injured; the sorrow of the bereaved. Comfort and relieve them, O merciful Father, according to their needs; for the sake of thy Son our Saviour Jesus Christ our Lord. [Attributed]

Sir Jacob Astley 1579–1652

Lord, thou knowest how busy I must be this day. If I forget thee, do not thou forget me, for Christ's sake.
[At the Battle of Edgehill, 1642]

St Augustine of Hippo 354–430

Watch thou, dear Lord, with those who wake, or watch, or weep tonight, and give thine angels charge over those who sleep. Tend the sick, O Lord Christ; rest the weary; bless the dying; soothe the suffering; shield the joyous; and all for thy love's sake.

O thou, from whom to be turned is to fall, to whom to be turned is to rise, and in whom to stand is to abide for ever;

Grant us in all our duties thy help, in all our perplexities thy guidance, in all our dangers thy protection, and in all our sorrows thy peace; through Jesus Christ our Lord.

Jane Austen 1775–1817

Incline us, O God! to think humbly of ourselves, to be saved only in the examination of our own conduct, to consider our fellow creatures with kindness, and to judge of all they say and do with the charity which we would desire from them ourselves.

William Bright 1824–1901

O God, who art Spirit, and willest to be worshipped in spirit and in truth: grant to us that, loving thee in all thoughts and above all things, we may please thee by our prayers and by our lives; through Jesus Christ our Lord.

Richard Baxter 1615–91

We thank thee for all thy mercies to our souls and bodies this night, and all our days and nights: for our rest and safety, and this morning's light. Cause us to spend this day in thy fear and faithful service. Preserve our souls from sin, and our bodies from all dangers or hurt which would hinder us from thy service. Cause us to live as in thy presence, and let us do all to please thee, and to thy glory, and to the good of our own souls and of one another: and let thy love, and praise, and service, be our continual delight; for Jesus Christ's sake, our Saviour and Intercessor at thy right hand.

St Benedict 480–543

O gracious and holy Father,
Give us wisdom to perceive thee,
intelligence to understand thee,
diligence to seek thee,
patience to wait for thee,
eyes to behold thee,
a heart to meditate upon thee,
and a life to proclaim thee;
through the power of the Spirit of Jesus Christ our Lord.

Motto of the Benedictine Order

Orare est laborare, laborare est orare
To pray is to work, to work is to pray.

William Blake 1757–1827

Jerusalem

And did those feet in ancient time
Walk upon England's mountains green?
And was the holy Lamb of God
On England's pleasant pastures seen?

And did the Countenance Divine
Shine forth upon our clouded hills?
And was Jerusalem builded here
Among these dark Satanic Mills?

Bring me my Bow of burning gold;
Bring me my Arrows of desire;
Bring me my Spear; O clouds unfold!
Bring me my Chariot of fire.

I will not cease from Mental Fight,
Nor shall my Sword sleep in my hand
Till we have built Jerusalem
In England's green and pleasant Land.

Phillips Brooks 1835–93

From *Sermons: Going Up to Jerusalem*

Do not pray for easy lives. Pray to be stronger men! Do not pray for tasks equal to your powers. Pray for powers equal to your tasks.

Sir Thomas Browne 1605–82

The night is come like to the day,
Depart not thou great God away.
Let not my sins, black as the night,
Eclipse the lustre of thy light.
Keep still in my horizon, for to me
The sun makes not the day, but thee.
Thou whose nature cannot sleep,
On my temples sentry keep;
Guard me 'gainst those watchful foes,
Whose eyes are open while mine close.
Let no dreams my head invest,
But such as Jacob's temples bless'd.
While I do rest, my soul advance,
Make my sleep a holy trance;
That I may, my rest being wrought,
Awake into some holy thought;
And with as active vigour run
My course, as doth the nimble sun.
Sleep is a death, O make me try
By sleeping what it is to die.
Howe'er I rest, great God, let me,
Awake again at last with thee.

Elizabeth Barrett Browning 1806–61

From *Aurora Leigh*

God answers sharp and sudden on some prayers,

And thrusts the thing we have prayed for in our face,
A gauntlet with a gift in 't. [*Book IV*]

Earth's crammed with heaven,
And every common bush afire with God. [*Book VII*]

ROBERT BURNS 1759–96

A Prayer in the Prospect of Death

1

O Thou unknown, Almighty Cause
  Of all my hope and fear!
In whose dread presence, ere an hour,
  Perhaps I must appear!

2

If I have wander'd in those paths
  Of life I ought to shun—
As something, loudly, in my breast
  Remonstrates I have done—

3

Thou know'st that Thou has formèd me
  With passions wild and strong;
And list'ning to their witching voice
  Has often led me wrong.

4

Where human weakness has come short,
  Or frailty stept aside,

Do Thou, All-good—for such Thou art—
   In shades of darkness hide.

5

Where with intention I have err'd,
   No other plea I have,
But, Thou art good; and Goodness still
   Delighteth to forgive.

Prayer: O Thou Dread Power

(Left in the room where he had slept while staying with a reverend friend)

1

O Thou dread Power, who reign'st above,
   I know thou wilt me hear,
When for this scene of peace and love
   I make my prayer sincere.

2

The hoary Sire—the mortal stroke,
   Long, long be pleas'd to spare:
To bless his little filial flock,
   And show what good men are.

3

She, who her lovely offspring eyes
   With tender hopes and fears—
O, bless her with a mother's joys,
   But spare a mother's tears!

4

Their hope, their stay, their darling youth,
  In manhood's dawning blush,
Bless him, Thou God of love and truth,
  Up to a parent's wish.

5

The beauteous, seraph sister-band—
  With earnest tears I pray—
Thou know'st the snares on every hand,
  Guide Thou their steps alway.

6

When, soon or late, they reach that coast,
  O'er Life's rough ocean driven,
May they rejoice, no wand'rer lost,
  A family in Heaven!

Prayer under the Pressure of Violent Anguish

1

O Thou Great Being! what Thou art
  Surpasses me to know;
Yet sure I am, that known to Thee
  Are all Thy works below.

2

Thy creature here before Thee stands,
  All wretched and distrest;
Yet sure those ills that wring my soul
  Obey Thy high behest.

3

Sure Thou, Almighty, canst not act
  From cruelty or wrath!
O, free my weary eyes from tears,
  Or close them fast in death!

4

But, if I must afflicted be,
  To suit some wide design,
Then man my soul with firm resolves
  To bear and not repine!

The Ninetieth Psalm Versified

1

O Thou, the first, the greatest friend
  Of all the human race!
Whose strong right hand has ever been
  Their stay and dwelling place!

2

Before the mountains heav'd their heads
  Beneath Thy forming hand,
Before this ponderous globe itself
  Arose at Thy command:

3

That Power, which rais'd and still upholds
  This universal frame,
From countless, unbeginning time
  Was ever still the same.

4

Those mighty periods of years,
  Which seem to us so vast,
Appear no more before Thy sight
  Than yesterday that's past.

5

Thou giv'st the word: Thy creature, man,
  Is to existence brought;
Again Thou say'st: 'Ye sons of Men,
  Return ye into nought!'

6

Thou layest them, with all their cares,
  In everlasting sleep;
As with a flood Thou tak'st them off
  With overwhelming sweep.

7

They flourish like the morning flower
  In beauty's pride array'd,
But long ere night, cut down, it lies
  All wither'd and decay'd.

Grace before Meat

Some hae meat and canna eat,
  And some would eat that want it;
But we hae meat and we can eat,
  Sae let the Lord be thankit.

A Grace before Dinner, Extempore

O Thou who kindly dost provide
  For every creature's want!
We bless Thee, God of Nature wide,
  For all Thy goodness lent:
And if it please Thee, heavenly Guide,
  May never worse be sent;
But whether granted or denied,
  Lord, bless us with content! Amen!

A Grace after Dinner, Extempore

O Thou, in whom we live and move—
  Who mad'st the sea and show;
Thy goodness constantly we prove,
  And, grateful, would adore:
And, if it please Thee, Power above!
  Still grant us, with such store,
The friend we trust, the fair we love—
  And we desire no more. Amen!

Extemporaneous Grace on a Haggis

(Expanded afterwards into 'Address to a Haggis')

Ye powers who give us a' that's guid,
Still bless auld Caledonia's brood
Wi' great John Barleycorn's heart's bluid,
    In stoups or luggies;
And on our board the king o' food,
    A glorious haggis!

Grace after Meat

Lord, we thank, and thee adore,
For temporal gifts we little merit;
At present we will ask no more
Let William Hislop* give the spirit.
(*William Hislop of the Globe Tavern)

GUY WETMORE CARRYL 1873–1904

From *When the Great Grey Ships Come in*

Thank God for peace! Thank God for peace,
when the great grey ships come in!

SAMUEL TAYLOR COLERIDGE 1772–1834

A Child's Evening Prayer

Ere on my bed my limbs I lay,
God grant me grace my prayers to say:
O God! preserve my mother dear
In strength and health for many a year;
And, O! preserve my father too,
And may I pay him reverence due;
And may I my best thoughts employ
To be my parents' hope and joy;
And, O! preserve my brothers both
From evil doings and from sloth,
And may we always love each others,
Our friends, our father, and our mother

And still, O Lord, to me impart
An innocent and grateful heart,
That after my last sleep I may
Awake to thy eternal day! Amen.

From *Hymn: Before Sunrise in the Vale of Chamouni*

Rise, O ever rise,
Rise like a cloud of incense, from the Earth!
Thou kingly Spirit throned among the hills,
Thou dread ambassador from Earth to Heaven,
Great hierarch! tell thou the silent sky,
And tell the stars, and tell yon rising sun,
Earth, with her thousand voices, praises God.

The Virgin's Cradle Hymn

(Copied from a print of the Virgin in a village in Germany)

Dormi, Jesu! Mater ridet
Quae tam dulcem somnum videt,
Dormi, Jesu! blandule!
Si non dormis, Mater plorat,
Inter fila cantans orat,
Blande, veni, somnule.
Sleep, sweet babe! my cares beguiling:
Mother sits beside thee smiling;
Sleep, my darling, tenderly!
If thou sleep not, mother mourneth,
Singing as her wheel she turneth:
Come, soft slumber, balmily!

From The Ancient Mariner

Farewell, farewell! but this I tell
To thee, thou Wedding Guest!
He prayeth well, who loveth well
Both man and bird and beast.

He prayeth best, who loveth best
All things both great and small;
For the dear God who loveth us,
He made and loveth all.

Bishop Cotton 1813–66

O God, who hast made of one blood all nations of men to dwell on the face of the earth, and didst send thy blessed Son, Jesus Christ, to preach peace to them that are far off, and to them that are night; grant that all the peoples of the world may feel after thee and find thee; and hasten, O Lord, the fulfilment of thy promise to pour out thy Spirit upon all flesh; through Jesus Christ our Lord.

John Donne 1572–1631

Eternal and most glorious God, who hast stamped the soul of man with thine Image, received it into thy Revenue, and made it a part of thy Treasure; suffer us not so to undervalue ourselfs, nay, so to impoverish thee, as to give away these souls for nothing, and all the world is nothing if the soul must be given for it. Do this, O God, for his sake who knows our natural infirmities, for he had them, and knows the weight of our sins, for he paid a dear price for them, thy Son our Saviour Jesus Christ.

Holy Sonnet

XIV

Batter my heart, three-person'd God; for, you
As yet but knock, breathe, shine, and seek to mend;
That I may rise, and stand, o'erthrow me, and bend
Your force, to break, blow, burn and make me new.
I, like an usurp'd town, to another due,
Labour to admit you, but Oh, to no end,
Reason your viceroy in me, me should defend,
But is captiv'd, and proves weak or untrue.
Yet dearly I love you, and would be loved fain,
But am betroth'd unto your enemy:
Divorce me, untie, or break that knot again,
Take me to you, imprison me, for I
Except you enthral me, never shall be free,
Nor ever chaste, except you ravish me.

A Hymn to God the Father

I

Wilt Thou forgive that sin where I begun
  Which is my sin, though it were done before?
Wilt Thou forgive that sin, through which I run,

And do run still: though still I do deplore?
When Thou hast done, Thou hast not done,
For, I have more.

II

Wilt Thou forgive that sin by which I have won
Others to sin? and, made my sin their door?
Wilt Thou forgive that sin which I did shun
A year, or two: but wallowed in, a score?
When Thou hast done, Thou hast not done,
For, I have more.

III

I have a sin of fear, that when I have spun
My last thread, I shall perish on the shore;
Swear by Thyself, that at my death Thy son
Shall shine as He shines now, and heretofore;
And, having done that, Thou hast done,
I fear no more.

JOHN ELLERTON 1826–93

From *Hymn*

The day thou gavest, Lord, is ended,
The darkness falls at thy behest;
To thee our morning hymns ascended,
Thy praise shall sanctify our rest.

So be it, Lord; thy throne shall never,
Like earth's proud empires, pass away:

Thy kingdom stands, and grows forever,
Till all thy creatures own thy sway.

Desiderius Erasmus 1466–1536

O Lord Jesus Christ, who art the Way, the Truth, and the Life, we pray thee suffer us not to stray from thee, who art the Way, nor to distrust thee, who art the Truth, nor to rest in any other thing than thee, who art the Life. Teach us by the Holy Spirit what to believe, what to do, and wherein to take our rest.

St Francis of Assissi 1181–1266

Lord, make us instruments of thy peace.
Where there is hatred let us sow love;
Where there is injury, pardon;
Where there is discord, union;
Where there is doubt, faith;
Where there is despair, hope;
Where there is darkness, light;
Where there is sadness, joy;
O Divine Master, grant that we may not so much seek to be consoled as to console; to be understood as to understand; to be loved, as to love; through the love of thy Son who died for us, Jesus Christ our Lord.

St Gregory 550–604

Almighty and everlasting God, with whom nothing is obscure, nothing dark, send forth thy light into our hearts that we may perceive the brightness of thy Law, and walking in thy holy way may fall into no sin, through thy beloved Son and our beloved example, Jesus Christ.

Pope Gregory XIII 1502–85

Ad maiorem Dei Gloriam
To the greater glory of God.
[Motto of the Society of Jesus]

Reginald Heber 1783–1826

Holy, Holy, Holy! Lord God Almighty!
Early in the morning our son shall rise to Thee:
Holy, Holy, Holy! Merciful and Mighty!
God in Three Persons, Blessed Trinity.

George Herbert 1593–1632

Discipline

Throw away Thy rod,
Throw away Thy wrath;
O my God,
Take the gentle path!

For my heart's desire
Unto Thine is bent:
I aspire
To a full consent.

Not a word or look
I affect to own,
        But by book,
And Thy Book alone.

Though I fail, I weep;
Though I halt in pace,
        Yet I creep
To the throne of grace.

Then let wrath remove;
Love will do the deed:
        For with love
Stony hearts will bleed.

Love is swift of foot;
Love's a man of war,
        And can shoot,
And can hit from far.

Who can 'scape his bow?
That which wrought on Thee,
        Brought Thee low,
Needs must work on me.

Throw away Thy rod;
Though man frailties hath,
        Thou art God:
Throw away Thy wrath!

Prayer (I)

Prayer the Church's banquet, Angels' age,
God's breath in man returning to his birth,
The soul in paraphrase, heart in pilgrimage,
The Christian plummet sounding heav'n and earth;
Engine against th' Almighty, sinners' tower,
Reversed thunder, Christ-side-piercing spear,
The six-days' world transposing in an hour,
A kind of tune, which all things hear and fear;
Softness, and peace, and joy, and love, and bliss,
Exalted Manna, gladness of the best,
Heaven in ordinary, man well drest,
The milky way, the bird of Paradise,
  Church bells beyond the stars heard, the soul's blood,
  The land of spices; something understood.

From *The Temple*

Who goes to bed and does not pray,
Maketh two nights to every day.

[*Charms and Knots*]

Teach me, my God and King
In all things thee to see
And what I do in any thing
To do it as for thee.

[*The Elixir*]

A servant with this clause
Makes drudgery divine:

Who sweeps a room, as for thy laws,
Makes that and th' action fine. [Ibid]

Thou who hast given so much to me,
Give one thing more, a grateful heart.

Robert Herrick 1591–1674

A Child's Grace

Here a little child I stand,
Heaving up my either hand;
Cold as paddocks though they be,
Here I lift them up to Thee,
For a benison to fall
On our meat, and on us all. Amen

[paddocks = toads]

Gerald Manley Hopkins 1844–89

Pied Beauty

Glory be to God for dappled things—
For skies of couple-colour as a brinded cow;
For rose-moles all in stipple upon trout that swim;
Fresch firecoal chestnut-falls; finches' wings;
Landscape plotted and piece—fold, fallow, and plough;
And, áll trádes, their gear and tackle and trim.

All things counter, original, spare, strange;
Whatever is fickle, freckled (who knows how?)
With swift, slow; sweet, sour; adazzle, dim;

He fathers-forth whose beauty is past change:
Praise him.

JOHN ANGELL JAMES 1785–1859

O Holy Spirit, the Comforter, come and dwell in our souls; make our bodies thy temple. Fill our minds with thy light, and our hearts with thy love, that over our whole character thy power may be seen in the beauties of holiness. May we live as something sacred to thee as well as perfected by thee. Come in all thy sevenfold energy, and replenish us with thy illuminating, comforting, sanctifying influence. Baptise us with celestial fire, and give us in thine abundant grace the earnest of glory everlasting.

THE JEWISH BLESSING *c.* 7TH CENTURY BC

The Lord bless us and keep us, the Lord make his face to shine upon us, and be gracious unto us, the Lord lift up the light of his countenance upon us and give us peace, now and evermore.

SAMUEL JOHNSON 1709–84

O Lord in whose hands are life and death, by whose power we are sustained, forgive us that we have suffered the days and hours, of which we must give account, to pass away without any endeavour to accomplish thy will. Make us to remember, O God, that every day is thy gift and ought to be used according to thy command. Grant us therefore so to repent of our negligence that we may pass the time which thou shalt yet allow us in diligent service; through Jesus Christ.

O God, who hast ordained that whatever is to be desired should be sought by labour, and who, by thy blessing, bringest honest labour to good effect: look with mercy upon our studies and endeavours. Grant us, O Lord, to design only what is lawful and right, and afford us calmness of mind and steadiness of purpose, that we may so do thy will in this short life as to obtain happiness in the world to come.

Almighty God, enlighten our understandings with knowledge of right that no deceit may mislead us, and govern our wills by thy laws that no temptation corrupt us; so may we also endeavour to do good and hinder evil. Amidst all the hopes and fears of this world, take not thy Holy Spirit from us, in the name of Christ our Lord.

Dame Julian of Norwich 1342–1413

God, of your goodness give me yourself for you are sufficient for me. I cannot properly ask anything less, to be worthy of you. If I were to ask less, I should always be in want. In you alone do I have all.

Bishop Thomas Ken 1637–1711

From *Doxology*

Praise God, from whom all blessings flow!
Praise Him, all creatures here below!
Praise Him above, ye heavenly host!
Praise Father, Son, and Holy Ghost!

Blessing and honour and thanksgiving and praise more than we can utter, more than we can conceive, be unto thee, O holy and glorious Trinity, Father, Son, and Holy Ghost, by all angels, all men, all creatures, for ever and ever.

O God, make the door of this house wide enough to receive all who need human love and fellowship, and a heavenly Father's care; and narrow enough to shut out all envy, pride and hate. Make its threshold smooth enough to be no stumbling block to children, nor to straying feet, but rugged enough to turn back the tempter's power: make it a gateway to thine eternal kingdom.

Charles Kingsley 1819–75

Take from us, O God,
All pride and vanity,
All boasting and forwardness;
And give us the true courage that shows itself by
gentleness,

The true wisdom that shows itself by simplicity,
And the true power that shows itself by modesty;
through Jesus Christ our Lord.

Abraham Lincoln 1809–65

Lord, give us faith that right makes might.

George Macdonald 1824–1905

O God of mountains, stars, and boundless spaces,
O God of freedom and of joyous hearts,
When thy face looketh forth from all men's faces,
There will be room enough in crowded marts!
Brood thou around me, and the noise is o'er,
Thy universe my closet with shut door.

Christopher Marlowe 1564–93

From *Dr Faustus*

O soul, be changed into little waterdrops,
And fall into the ocean—ne'er to be found.
My God! My God! look not so fierce on me!

Sir Thomas More 1478–1535

These things, good Lord, that we pray for, give us thy grace to labour for.

Prayer from The New England Primer

Now I lay me down to sleep,

I pray thee, Lord, my soul to keep;
If I should die before I wake,
I pray thee, Lord, my soul to take.

John Henry Newman, 1801-90

Praise to the Holiest in the height,
And in the depth be praise;
In all his words most wonderful,
Most sure in all his ways.

O loving wisdom of our God!
When all was sin and shame,
A second Adam to the fight
And to the rescue came.

O wisest love! that flesh and blood,
Which did in Adam fail,
Should strive afresh against the foe,
Should strive and should prevail;

And that a higher gift than grace
Should flesh and blood refine,
God's presence and his very self,
And essence all-divine.

O generous love! that he who smote
In Man, for man, the foe,
The double agony in Man,
For man, should undergo;

And in the garden secretly,
  And on the cross on high,
Should teach his brethren, and inspire
  To suffer and to die.

Praise to the Holiest in the height,
  And in the depth be praise;
In all his words most wonderful,
  Most sure in all his ways.

Prayers from the New Testament

Matthew 5:44–45

Love your enemies, bless them that curse you, do good to them that hate you, and pray for them which despitefully use you, and persecute you; That ye may be the children of your Father which is in heaven: for he maketh his sun to rise on the evil and on the good, and sendeth rain on the just and on the unjust.

Matthew 6:5–13

And when thou prayest, thou shalt not be as the hypocrites are; for they love to pray standing in the synagogues and in the corners of the streets, that they may be seen of men. Verily I say unto you, They have their reward. But thou, when thou prayest, enter into thy closet, and when thou hast shut thy door, pray to thy Father which is in secret; and thy Father which seeth in secret shall reward thee openly. But when ye pray, use no vain repetitions, as the heathen do: for they think that they shall be heard for their much speaking. Be not ye therefore like unto them: for your Father knoweth what things ye have need of, before ye ask him. After this manner therefore pray ye: Our Father which art in heave, Hallowed be thy name. Thy kingdom come. Thy will be done in earth, as it is in heaven. Give us this day our daily bread. And forgive us our debts, as we forgive our debtors. And lead us not into temptation, but deliver us from evil: For thine is the kingdom, and the power, and the glory, for ever. Amen.

Matthew 7:7–12

Ask, and it shall be given you; seek, and ye shall find; knock, and it shall be opened unto you. For every one that asketh receiveth; and he that seeketh findeth; and to him that knocketh it shall be opened. Or what man is there of you, whom if his son ask bread, will he give him a stone? Or if he ask a fish, will he give him a serpent? If ye then, being evil, know how to give good gifts unto your children, how much more shall your Father which is in heaven give good things to them that ask him? Therefore all things whatsoever ye would that men should do to you, do ye even so to them.

Matthew 26:41

Watch and pray, that ye enter not into temptation: the spirit indeed is willing but the flesh is weak.

Mark 11:24–26

Therefore I say unto you, What things soever ye desire, when ye pray, believe that ye receive them, and ye shall have them. And when ye stand praying, forgive, if ye have ought against any: that your Father also which is in heaven may forgive you your trespasses. But if ye do not forgive, neither will your Father which is in heaven forgive your trespasses.

Mark 13:33

Take ye heed, watch and pray: for ye know not when the time is.

Luke 2:14

Glory to God in the highest, and on earth peace, good will toward men.

Luke 11:1–4

And it came to pass, that, as he was praying in a certain place, when he ceased, one of his disciples said unto him, Lord, teach us to pray, as John also taught his disciples. And he said unto them, When ye pray, say, Our Father which art in heaven, Hallowed be thy name. Thy kingdom come. Thy will be done, as in heaven, so in earth. Give us day by day our daily bread. And forgive us our sins; for we also forgive every one that is indebted to us. And lead us not into temptation; but deliver us from evil.

John 3:16

For God so loved the world that he gave his only begotten Son, that whosoever believeth in him should not perish, but have everlasting life.

John 14:13–16

And whatsoever ye shall ask in my name, that will I do, that the Father may be glorified in the Son. If ye shall ask anything in my name, I will do it. If ye love me, keep my commandments. And I will pray the Father, and he shall give you another Comforter, that hey may abide with you for ever.

2 Corinthians 13:14

The grace of the Lord Jesus Christ, and the love of God, and the communion of the Holy ghost, be with you all. Amen.

Philippians 4:6–9

Be careful for nothing; but in every thing by prayer and supplication with thanksgiving let your requests be made known unto God. And the peace of God, which passeth all understanding, shall keep your hearts and minds through Christ Jesus. Finally, brethren, whatsoever things are true, whatsoever things are honest, whatsoever things are just, whatsoever things are pure, whatsoever things are lovely, whatsoever things are of good report; if there be any virtue, and if there be any praise, think on these things. Those things, which ye have both learned, and received, and heard, and seen in me, do: and the God of peace shall be with you.

1 Thessalonians 5:16–18

Rejoice evermore. Pray without ceasing. In every thing give thanks: for this is the will of God in Christ Jesus concerning you.

2 Thessalonians 3:1

Pray for us, that the word of the Lord may have free course, and be glorified, even as it is with you.

1 Timothy 1:17

Now unto the King eternal, immortal, invisible, the only wise God, be honour and glory for ever and ever. Amen.

James 5:15–16

And the prayer of faith shall save the sick, and the Lord shall raise him up; and if he have committed sins, they shall be forgiven him. Confess your faults one to another, and pray one for another, that ye may be healed. The effectual fervent prayer of a righteous man availeth much.

1 John 5:13–15

These things have I written unto you that believe on the name of the Son of God; that ye may know that ye have eternal life, and that ye may believe on the name of the Son of God. And this is the confidence that we have in him, that, if we ask any thing according to his will, he heareth us: And if we know that he hear us, whatsoever we ask, we know that we have the petitions that we desired of him.

Jude 24–25

Now unto him that is able to keep you from falling, and to present you faultless before the presence of his glory with exceeding joy. To the only wise God our Saviour, be glory and majesty, dominion and power, both now and ever. Amen.

St Patrick 389–461

Christ be with me, Christ within me,
Christ behind me, Christ before me,
Christ beside me, Christ to win me,
Christ to comfort and restore me.
Christ beneath me, Christ above me,
Christ in quiet, Christ in danger,
Christ in heart of all that love me,
Christ in mouth of friend and stranger.

May the strength of God pilot us.
May the power of God preserve us.
May the wisdom of God instruct us.
May the hand of God protect us.
May the way of God direct us.

May the shield of God defend us.
May the host of God guard us against the snares of evil and the temptations of the world.
May Christ be with us, Christ before us, Christ in us, Christ over us.
May thy salvation, O Lord, be always ours this day and for evermore.

William Penn 1644–1718

O God, help us not to despise or oppose what we do not understand; through Jesus Christ our Lord.

Samuel Pepys 1633–1703

I pray God to keep me from being proud.

[*Diary* 22 March 1660]

This morning came home my fine camlet cloak, with gold buttons, and a silk suit, which cost me much money, and I pray God to make me able to pay for it.

[Ibid 1 July 1660]

Pericles 495–429 BC

O God, grant that no word may fall from us, against our will, unfit for the present need.

Prayers from the Psalms

Psalm 8

O Lord our Lord, how excellent is thy name in all the earth! Who hast set thy glory above the heavens. Out of the mouth of babes and sucklings hast thou ordained strength because of thine enemies, that thou mightest still the enemy and the avenger. When I consider thy heavens, the work of thy finger, the moon and the stars, which thou hast ordained; What is man, that thou art mindful of him? and the son of man, that thou visitest him? For thou hast made him a little lower than the angels, and hast crowned him with glory and honour. Thou madest him to have dominion over the works of thy hands; thou hast put all things under his feet: All sheep and oxen, yea, and the beasts of the field; The fowl of the air, and the fish of the sea, and whatsoever passeth through the paths of the seas. O Lord our Lord, how excellent is thy name in all the earth!

Psalm 23

The Lord is my shepherd; I shall not want. He maketh me to lie down in green pastures: he leadeth me beside the still waters. He restoreth my soul: he leadeth me in the paths of righteousness for his name's sake. Yea, though I walk through the valley of the shadow of death, I will fear no evil: for thou art with me; thy rod and thy staff they comfort me. Thou preparest a table before me in the presence of mine enemies: thou anointest my head with oil; my cup runneth over. Surely goodness and mercy shall follow me all the days of my life: and I will dwell in the house of the Lord for ever.

Psalm 34:1–3

I will bless the Lord at all times: his praise shall continually be in my mouth. My soul shall make her boast in the Lord: the humble shall hear thereof, and be glad. O magnify the Lord with me, and let us exalt his name together.

Psalm 61:1–5

Hear my cry, O God; attend unto my prayer. From the end of the earth will I cry unto thee, when my heart is overwhelmed: lead me to the rock that is higher than I. For thou hast been a shelter for me, and a strong tower from the enemy. I will abide in thy tabernacle for ever: I will trust in the cover of thy wings. Selah. For thou, O God, hast heard my vows: thou hast given me the heritage of those that fear thy name.

Psalm 67

God be merciful unto us, and bless us; and cause his face to shine upon us; Selah. That thy way may be known upon earth, thy saving health among all nations. Let the people praise thee, O God; let all the people praise thee. O let the nations be glad and sing for joy: for thou shalt judge the people righteously, and govern the nations upon earth. Selah. Let the people praise thee, O God; let all the people praise thee. Then shall the earth yield her increase; and God, even our own God, shall bless us. God shall bless us; and all the ends of the earth shall fear him.

Psalm 103:1–6

Bless the Lord, O my soul: and all that is within me, bless his holy name. Bless the Lord, O my soul, and forget not all his benefits: Who forgiveth all thine iniquities; who healeth all thy diseases; Who reedeemeth thy life from destruction; who crowneth thee with loving kindness and tender mercies; Who satisfieth thy mouth with good things; so that thy youth is renewed like the eagle's. The Lord executeth righteousness and judgment for all that are oppressed.

Psalm 104:1–8

Bless the Lord, O my soul. O Lord my God, thou art very great; thou art clothed with honour and majesty. Who coverest thyself with light as with a garment: who stretchest out the heavens like a curtain: Who layeth the beams of his chambers in the waters: who maketh the clouds his chariot: who walketh upon the wings of the wind: Who maketh his angels spirits; his ministers a flaming fire: Who laid the foundations of the earth, that it should not be removed for ever. Thou coverest it with the deep as with a garment: the waters stood above he mountains. At thy rebuke they fled; at the voice of thy thunder they hasted away. They go up by the mountains; they go down by the valleys unto the place which thou hast founded for them.

Psalm 104:33–35

I will sing unto the Lord as long as I live: I will sing praise to my God while I have my being. My meditation of him shall be sweet: I will be glad in the Lord. Let the sinners be consumed out of the earth, and let the wicked be no more. Bless thou the Lord, O my soul. Praise ye the Lord.

Psalm 113: 1–3

Praise ye the Lord, Praise, O ye servants of the Lord, praise the name of the Lord. Blessed be the name of the Lord from this time forth and for evermore. From the rising of the sun unto the going down of the same the Lord's name is to be praised.

Psalm 121

I will lift up mine eyes unto the hills, from whence cometh my help. My help cometh from the Lord, which made heaven and earth. He will not suffer thy foot to be moved: he that keepeth thee will not slumber. Behold, he that keepeth Israel shall neither slumber nor sleep. The Lord is thy keeper: the Lord is thy shade upon thy right hand. The sun shall not smite thee by day, nor the moon by night. The Lord shall preserve thee from all evil: he shall preserve thy soul. The Lord shall preserve thy going out and thy coming in from this time forth, and even for evermore.

Psalm 123

Unto thee lift I up mine eyes, O thou that dwellest in

the heavens. Behold, as the eyes of servants look unto the hand of their masters, and as the eyes of a maiden unto the hand of her mistress; so our eyes wait upon the Lord our God, until that he have mercy upon us. Have mercy upon us. Have mercy upon us, O Lord, have mercy upon us: for we are exceedingly filled with contempt. Our soul is exceedingly filled with the scorning of those that are at ease, and with the contempt of the proud.

Psalm 130:1–6

Out of the depths have I cried unto thee, O Lord. Lord, hear my voice; let thine ears be attentive to the voice of my supplications. If thou, Lord, shouldest mark iniquities, O Lord, who shall stand? But there is forgiveness with thee, that thou mayest be feared. I wait for the Lord, my soul doth wait, and in his word do I hope. My soul waiteth for the Lord more than they that watch for the morning: I say, more than they that watch for the morning.

Psalm 148:7–13

Praise the Lord from the earth, ye dragons, and all deeps: Fire, and hail: snow, and vapours; stormy wind fulfilling his word: Mountains, and all hills; fruitful trees, and all cedars: Beasts, and all cattle; creeping things, and flying fowl: Kings of the earth, and all people; princes, and all judges of the earth: Both young men, and maidens; old men, and children: Let them praise the name of the Lord: for his name alone is excellent; his glory is above the earth and heaven.

Psalm 150

Praise ye the Lord. Praise God in his sanctuary: praise him in the firmament of his power. Praise him for his mighty acts: praise him according to his excellent greatness. Praise him with the sound of the trumpet: praise him with the psaltery and harp. Praise him with the timbrel and dance: praise him with stringed instruments and organs. Praise him upon the loud cymbals: praise him upon the high sounding cymbals. Let every thing that hath breath praise the Lord. Praise ye the Lord.

Francis Quarles 1592–1644

Thou art my Life; if thou but turn away,
My life's a thousand deaths; thou art my Way;
Without thee, Lord, I travel not, but stray.

My light thou art; without thy glorious sight
My eyes are darkened with perpetual night:
My God, thou art my Way, my Life, my Light.

St Richard of Chichester 1197–1253

Thanks be to thee, my Lord Jesus Christ,
for all the benefits which thou hast given me,
for all the pains and insults which thou hast borne for me:

O most merciful Redeemer, Friend and Brother;
may I know thee more clearly,
love thee more dearly,
follow thee more nearly,
day by day.

Bishop Ridley *c.*1500–55

Lord, for thy tender mercy's sake, lay not our sins to our charge, but forgive that is past and give us grace to amend our lives; to decline from sin and incline to virtue, that we may walk with a perfect heart before thee, now and evermore.

Wentworth Dillon, Earl of Roscommon *c.*1633–84

My God, my Father, and my Friend,
Do not forsake me in my end.

Christina Rossetti 1830–94

Sweet Death

The sweetest blossoms die.
And so it was that, going day by day
Unto the Church to praise and pray,
And crossing the green churchyard thoughtfully,
I saw how on the graves the flowers
Shed their fresh leaves in showers,
And how their perfume rose up to the sky
Before it passed away.

The youngest blossoms die.
  They die and fall and nourish the rich earth
  From which they lately had their birth;
Sweet life, but sweeter death that passeth by
  And is as though it had not been—
  All colours turn to green;
The bright hues vanish and the odours fly,
  The grass hath lasting worth.

And youth and beauty die.
  So be it, O my God, Thou God of Truth:
  Better than beauty and than youth
Are Saints and Angels, a glad company;
  And Thou, O Lord, our Rest and Ease,
  Art better far than these.
Why should we shrink from our full harvest why
  Prefer to glean with Ruth?

The Sarum Primer Prayer

God be in my head, and in my understanding;
God be in my eyes, and in my looking;
God be in my mouth, and in my speaking;
God be in my heart, and in my thinking;
God be at mine end, and at my departing.

William Shakespeare

O Lord, that lends us life,
Lend us a heart replete with thankfulness.

[*King Henry VI*]

Go with me, like good angels, to my end;
And, as the long divorce of steel falls on me,
Make of your payers one sweet sacrifice,
And lift my soul to heaven. [*King Henry VIII*]

Percy Bysshe Shelley

Ode to Heaven

Chorus of Spirits
First Spirit
Palace-roof of cloudless nights!
Paradise of golden lights!
  Deep, immeasurable, vast,
Which art now, and which were then
  Of the present and the past,
Of the eternal where and when,
  Presence-chamber, temple, home,
  Ever-canopying dome,
  Of acts and ages yet to come!

Glorious shapes have life in thee,
Earth, and all earth's company;
  Living globes which ever throng
Thy deep chasms and wildernesses;
  And green worlds that glide along;
And swift stars with flashing tresses;
  And icy moons most cold and bright,
  And mighty suns beyond the night
  Atoms of intensest light.

Even thy name is as a god,
Heaven! for thou art the abode
  Of that power which is the glass
Wherein man his nature sees.
  Generations as they pass
Worship thee with bended knees.
  Their unremaining gods and they
  Like a river roll away:
  Thou remainest such alway.

Second Spirit
Thou art but the mind's first chamber,
Round which its young fancies clamber,
  Like weak insects in a cave,
Lighted up by stalactites;
  But the portal of the grave,
Where a world of new delights
  Will make thy best glories seem
  But a dim and noonday gleam
  From the shadow of a dream!

Third Spirit
Peace! the abyss is wreathed with scorn
At your presumption, atom-born!
  What is heaven? and what are yet
Who its brief expanse inherit?
  What are suns and spheres which flee
With he instinct of that spirit
  Of which ye are but a part?

Drops which Nature's mighty heart
Drives through thinnest veins! Depart!

What is heaven? a globe of dew,
Filling in the morning new
Some eyed flower whose young leaves waken
On an unimagined world:
Constellated suns unshaken,
Orbits measureless, are furled
In that frail and fading sphere,
With ten millions gathered there,
To tremble, gleam, and disappear.

Christopher Smart 1722–71

For adoration seasons change,
and order, truth, and beauty range,
Adjust, attract, and fill:
The grass thc polyanthus cheques;
And polish'd porphyry reflects,
By the descending rill.

Rich almonds colour to the prime
For adoration; tendrils climb,
And fruit-trees pledge their gems;
And Ivis, with her gorgeous vest,
Builds for her eggs her cunning nest,
And bell-flowers bow their stems.

Now labour his reward receives,

For adoration counts his sheaves,
   To peace, her bounteous prince;
The nectarine his strong tint imbibes,
And apples of ten thousand tribes,
   And quick peculiar quince.

Robert Louis Stevenson 1850–94

The Celestial Surgeon

If I have faltered more or less
In my great task of happiness;
If I have moved among my race
And shown no glorious morning face;
If beams from happy human eyes
Have moved me not; if morning skies,
Books, and my food, and summer rain
Knocked on my sullen heart in vain—
Lord, Thy most pointed pleasure take
And stab my spirit broad awake;
Or, Lord, if too obdurate I,
Choose Thou, before that spirit die,
A piercing pain, a killing sin,
And to my dead heart run them in!

Prayer

I ask good things that I detest,
   With speeches fair;
Heed not, I pray thee, Lord, my breast,
   But hear my prayer.

I say ill things I would not say—
  Things unaware:
Regard my breast, Lore, in Thy day,
  And not my prayer.

My heart is evil in Thy sight:
  My good thoughts flee:
O Lord, I cannot wish aright—
  Wish Thou for me.

O bend my words and acts to Thee,
  However ill,
That I, what e'er I say or be,
  May serve Thee still.

O let my thoughts abide in Thee
  Lest I should fall:
Show me Thyself in all I see,
  Thou Lord of all.

CLIV

Since Thou hast given me this good hope, O God,
That while my footsteps tread the flowery sod
And the great woods embower me, and white dawn
And purple even sweetly lead me on
From day to day and night to night, O God,
My life shall no wise miss the light of love,
But ever climbing, climb above
Man's one poor star, man's supine lands,
Into the azure steadfastness of death.

My life shall no wise lack the light of love,
My hands not lack the loving touch of hands,
But day by day unto my last of years,
I shall be one that has a perfect friend,
Her heart shall taste my laughter and my tears,
And her kind eyes shall lead me to the end.

Prayer for Success

Lord, behold our family here assembled. We thank Thee for this place in which we dwell; for the love that unites us; for the peace accorded us this day; for the hope with which we expect the morrow; for the health, the work, the food, and the bright skies, that make our lives delightful; for our friends in all parts of the earth, and our friendly helpers in this foreign isle. Let peace abound in our small company. Purge out of every heart the lurking grudge. Give us grace and strength to forbear and to persevere. Offenders, give us the grace to accept and to forgive offenders. Forgetful ourselves, help us to bear cheerfully the forgetfulness of others. Give us courage and gaiety and the quiet mind. Spare to us our friends, soften to us our enemies. Bless us, if it may be, in all our innocent endeavours. If it may not, give us the strength to encounter that which is to come, that we be brave in peril, constant in tribulation, temperate in wrath, and in all changes of fortune, and, down to the gates of death, loyal and loving one to another. As the clay to the potter, as the windmill to the wind, as children of their sire, we beseech of Thee this help and mercy for Christ's sake.

Prayer for Grace

Grant that we here before Thee may be set free from the fear of vicissitude and the fear of death, may finish what remains before us of our course without dishonour to ourselves or hurt to others, and, when the day comes, may die in peace. Deliver us from fear and favour: from mean hopes and cheap pleasures. Have mercy on each in his deficiency; let him be not cast down; support the stumbling on the way, and give at last rest to the weary.

Prayer at Morning

The day returns and brings us the petty round of irritating concerns and duties. Help us to play the man, help us to perform them with laughter and kind faces, let cheerfulness abound with industry. Give us to go blithely on our business all this day, bring us to our resting beds weary and content and undishonoured, and grant us in the end the gift of sleep.

Evening Prayer

We come before Thee, O Lord, in the end of the day with thanksgiving.

Our beloved in the far parts of the earth, those who

are now beginning the labours of the day what time we end them, and those with whom the sun now stands at the point of noon, bless, help, console, and prosper them.

Our guard is relieved, the service of the day is over, and the hour come to rest. We resign into thy hands our sleeping bodies, our cold hearths, and open doors. Give us to awake with smiles, give us to labour smiling. As the sun returns in the east, so let our patience be renewed with dawn; as the sun lightens the world, so let our loving kindness make bright this house of our habitation.

Another For The Evening

Lord, receive our supplications for this house, family, and country. Protect the innocent, restrain the greedy and the treacherous, lead us out of our tribulation into a quiet land.

Look down upon ourselves and upon our absent dear ones. Help us and them; prolong our days in peace and honour. Give us health, food, bright weather, and light hearts. In what we meditate of evil, frustrate our will; in what of good, further our endeavours. Cause injuries to be forgot and benefits to be remembered.

Let us lie down without fear and awake and arise with exultation. For his sake, in whose words we now conclude.

In Time Of Rain

We thank Thee, Lord, for the glory of the late days and the excellent face of thy sun. We thank Thee for good news received. We thank Thee for the pleasures we have enjoyed and for those we have been able to confer. And now, when the clouds gather and the rain impends over the forest and our house, permit us not to be cast down; let us not lose the savour of past mercies and past pleasures; but, like the voice of a bird singing in the rain, let grateful memory survive in the hour of darkness. If there be in front of us any painful duty, strengthen us with the grace of courage; if any act of mercy, teach us tenderness and patience.

Another In Time Of Rain

Lord, Thou sendest down rain upon the uncounted millions of the forest, and givest the trees to drink exceedingly. We are here upon this isle a few handfuls of men, and how many myriads upon myriads of stalwart trees! Teach us the lesson of the trees. The sea around us, which this rain recruits, teems with the race of fish; teach us, Lord, the meaning of the fishes. Let us see ourselves for what we are, one out of the countless number of the clans of thy handiwork. When we would despair, let us remember that these also please and serve Thee.

Before A Temporary Separation

Today we go forth separate, some of us to pleasure, some of us to worship, some upon duty. Go with us, our guide and angel; hold Thou before us in our divided paths the mark of our low calling, still to be true to what small best we can attain to. Help us in that, our maker, the dispenser of events—Thou, of the vast designs, in which we blindly labour, suffer us to be so far constant to ourselves and our beloved.

For Friends

For our absent loved ones we implore thy loving-kindness. Keep them in life, keep them in growing honour; and for us, grant that we remain worthy of their love. For Christ's sake, let not our beloved blush for us, nor we for them. Grant us but that, and grant us courage to endure lesser ills unshaken, and to accept death, loss, and disappointment as it were straws upon the tide of life.

For The Family

Aid us, if it be thy will, in our concerns. Have mercy on this land and innocent people. Help them who this day contend in disappointment with their frailties. Bless our family, bless our forest house, bless our island helpers. Thou who hast made for us this place of ease and hope, accept and inflame our gratitude;

help us to repay, in service one to another, the debt of thine unmerited benefits and mercies, so that, when the period of our stewardship draws to a conclusion, when the windows begin to be darkened, when the bond of the family is to be loosed, there shall be no bitterness of remorse in our farewells.

Help us to look back on the long way that Thou hast brought us, on the long days in which we have been served, not according to our deserts, but our desires; on the pit and the miry clay, the blackness of despair, the horror of misconduct, from which our feet have been plucked out. For our sins forgiven or prevented, for our shame unpublished, we bless and thank Thee, O God. Help us yet again and ever. So order events, so strengthen our frailty, as that day by day we shall come before Thee with this song of gratitude, and in the end we be dismissed with honour. In their weakness and their fear, the vessels of thy handiwork so pray to Thee, so praise Thee. Amen.

Sunday

We beseech Thee, Lord, to behold us with fav[illegible] of many families and nations gathered toget[illegible] peace of this roof, weak men and women subsisting under the covert of thy patience. Be patient still; suffer us yet awhile longer; with our broken purposes of good, with our idle endeavours against evil, suffer us awhile longer to endure, and (if it may be) help us to do better. Bless to us our extraordinary mercies; if the day come when these must be taken, brace us to play the man under affliction. Be with our friends, be with ourselves. Go with each of us to rest; if any awake, temper to them the dark hours of watching; and when the day returns, return to us, our sun and comforter, and call us up with morning faces and with morning hearts—eager to labour—eager to be happy, if happiness shall be our portion and if the day be marked for sorrow, strong to endure it.

We thank Thee and praise Thee; and in the words of him to whom this day is sacred, close our oblation.

For Self-Blame

Lord, enlighten us to see the beam that is in our own eye, and blind us to the mote that is in our brother's. Let us feel our offences with our hands, make them great and bright before us like the sun, make us eat them and drink them for our diet. Blind us to the offences of our beloved, cleanse them from our memories, take them out of our mouths for ever. Let [illegible] ore Thee carry and measure with the false [illegible] love, and be in their own eyes and in all conjunctures the most guilty. Help us at the same time with the grace of courage, that we be none of us cast down when we sit lamenting amid the ruins of our happiness or our integrity: touch us with fire from the altar, that we may be up and doing to rebuild our city: in the name and by the method of him in whose words of prayer we now conclude.

For Self-Forgetfulness

Lord, the creatures of thy hand, thy disinherited children, come before Thee with their incoherent wishes and regrets: Children we are, children we shall be, till our mother the earth hath fed upon our bones. Accept us, correct us, guide us, thy guilty innocents. Dry our vain tears, wipe out our vain resentments, help our yet vainer efforts. If there be any here, sulking as children will, deal with and enlighten him. Make it day about that person, so that he shall see himself and be ashamed. Make it heaven about him, Lord, by the only way to heaven, forgetfulness of self, and make it day about his neighbours, so that they shall help, not hinder him.

For Renewal of Joy

We are evil, O God, and help us to see it and amend. We are good, and help us to be better. Look down upon thy servants with a patient eye, even as Thou sendest sun and rain; look down, call upon the dry bones, quicken, enliven; recreate in us the soul of service, the spirit of peace; renew in us the sense of joy.

Jonathan Swift 1667–1745

From Polite Conversation

I always love to begin a journey on Sundays, because I shall have the prayers of the church to preserve all that travel by land, or by water.

Thomas à Kempis 1380–1471

Grant us, O Lord, to know that which is worth knowing, to love that which is worth loving, to praise that which can bear with praise, to hate what in thy sight is unworthy, to prize what to thee is precious, and, above all, to search out and to do what is well-pleasing unto thee; through Jesus Christ our Lord.

We offer unto Thee our prayers and intercessions, for those especially who have in any matter hurt, grieved or found fault with us or who have done us any damage or displeasure.

For all those also whom, at any time, we have vexed, troubled, burdened, and scandalized, by words or deeds, knowingly or in ignorance: that Thou wouldst grant us all equally pardon for our sins, and for our offences against each other.

Take away from our hearts, O Lord, all suspiciousness, indignation, wrath and contention, and whatsoever may hurt charity, and lessen brotherly love. Have mercy, O Lord, have mercy on those that crave thy mercy, give grace unto them that stand in need thereof, and make us such that we may be worthy to enjoy Thy grace, and go forward to life eternal.

Thomas Aquinas 1225–74

Give us, O Lord, a steadfast heart, which no unworthy affection may drag downwards; give us an unconquered heart, which no tribulation can wear out; give us an upright heart, which no unworthy purpose may tempt aside. Bestow upon us also, O Lord our God, understanding to know thee, diligence to seek thee, wisdom to find thee, and a faithfulness that may finally embrace thee; through Jesus Christ our Lord.

God of all goodness, grant us to desire ardently, to seek wisely, to know surely, and to accomplish perfectly thy holy will, for the glory of thy name.

Dean Vaughan 1816–97

O loving Father, our eternal friend, may we never forget or dishonour thee this day; but in all things and in all occupations remember thy presence and cherish thy love; for Jesus Christ's sake.

Voltaire [François Marie Arouet] 1694–1778

I have never made but one prayer to God, a very short one: "O Lord, make my enemies ridiculous." And God granted it. [From a letter written in 1767]

William I (William the Silent) 1533–84

Mon Dieu, ayez pitié de mon âme et de mon pauvre peuple
My God, have mercy on my soul and on my poor people. [Last words on his assassination]

Thomas Wilson 1663–1755

Forgive me my sins, O Lord—the sins of my present and the sins of my past, the sins of my soul and the sins of my body, the sins which I have done to please myself and the sins which I have done to please others. Forgive me my casual sins and my deliberate sins and those which I have laboured so to hide that I have hidden them even from myself. Forgive me them, O Lord, forgive them all; for Jesus Christ's sake.

William Wordsworth 1770–1850

From the Italian of Michael Angelo. To the Supreme Being

The prayers I make will then be sweet indeed
If Thou the spirit give by which I pray:
My unassisted heart is barren clay,
That of its native self can nothing feed:
Of good and pious works Thou art the seed,
That quickens only where Thou say'st it may:
Unless Thou show to us thine own true way

No man can find it: Father! Thou must lead.
Do Thou, then, breathe those thoughts into my mind
By which such virtue may in me be bred
That in thy holy footsteps I may tread;
The fetters of my tongue do Thou unbind,
That I may have the power to sing of Thee,
and sound thy praises everlastingly.

Hymn for the boatmen, as they approach the rapids under the castle of Heidelberg

Jesu! bless our slender boat,
By the current swept along;
Loud its threatenings—let them not
Drown the music of a song
Breathed Thy mercy to implore,
Where these troubled waters roar!

Saviour, for our warning, seen
Bleeding on that precious Rood;
If, while through the meadows green
Gently wound the peaceful flood,
We forget Thee, do not Thou
Disregard Thy Suppliants now!

Hither, like yon ancient Tower
watching o'er the river's bed,
Fling the shadow of thy power,
Else we sleep among the dead;

Thou who trod'st the billowy sea,
Shield us in our jeopardy!

Guide our bark among the waves;
    Through the rocks our passage smooth;
Where the whirlpool frets and raves
    Let thy love its anger soothe:
All our hope is placed in Thee;
    Miserere Domine!